Copyright Nr

Table of Contents

1 Introduction

Christmas is a very special holiday not only in Germany but all over the world. We Germans value traditions very much, and Christmas reminds us of our childhood.

It's such a special time of year. Longstanding traditions and customs like decorating your home, baking cookies (Weihnachtsplätzchen) and visiting the Christmas markets with your friends are some of my favorite Christmas traditions.

Whether you're an active Christian or not, the magic atmosphere of December and the holiday season gets to everyone. This is the time when the days become shorter, darkness sets in by late afternoon and days get colder; it may even start snowing, just in time for Christmas.

For us Germans a white Christmas with snowflakes falling is still the epitome of a perfect holiday. Every year, we anxiously await the first snow in December and hope for it to last at least until the day after Christmas. Even though we cannot influence the weather, there are lots of other things we can do to make the holiday season the most joyous time of the year.

Please read on as I take you on a journey through many German Christmas traditions filled with happy memories from my childhood.

2　Advent

Officially, the holiday starts with the first Advent, even though nowadays, you can buy Christmas decorations and cookies much earlier, as early as the beginning of October.

Advent (derived form the Latin word adventus, which means arrival) is the time for preparing for the arrival of Jesus. It starts with the fourth Sunday before Christmas Eve, usually at the end of November or beginning of December. These are the dates for the next four first Advent Sundays.

1. Advent 2021: Sunday, 28.11.2021

1. Advent 2022: Sunday, 27.11.2022

1. Advent 2023: Sunday, 3.12.2023

1.Advent 2024: Sunday, 1.12.2024

In the Christian tradition this is the time to slow down your busy lives and prepare mentally and spiritually for the arrival of Jesus Christ.

Nowadays, the religious meaning has moved to the background, and Advent is mainly the time for gift shopping and lots of

Christmas parties. It's a nice custom that companies reward their employees for a year of faithful service with a dinner or similar activity in December.

Families and friends have get-togethers, and about every club or community uses December to close-down the year with some kind of festivity.

The Saturdays in December (Adventssamstag) are the days when everyone flocks to the big shopping areas in any major German city to take in the Christmas atmosphere, visit the Christmas markets and do their gift shopping. You will literally join thousands of co-shoppers and crowd the stores. As a side note, one of my friends who works in a soap shop, told me that almost 90 percent of the year's sales are made in December. Now you get the idea about how crowded it is.

But this shouldn't alienate you. Even though almost everyone complains (including me), we still dive into the crowds and seem to enjoy it after all. I will get to the famous German Christmas markets in a later chapter; for now let's talk about two of my favorite Advent traditions.

2.1 Advent Wreath - Adventskranz

We Germans love to decorate our homes with Christmas things! One of our favorite decorations are candles in all forms and sizes and the wreath even has four of them, one for each Sunday in Advent.

The Advent wreath is made of real or artificial fir branches and decorated with apples, fir cones, little berries or whatever else you may think of and finally topped with four candles. It's believed that Johann Wichern introduced this tradition as early as 1839.

You can buy an *Adventskranz* in basically every major department store, as well as in crafts and flower shops. Cheap plastic ones start as low as 10 Euro up to hand-made ones with wonderfully ornamented candles for up to 100 Euro.

In my childhood we used to go into the forest (I lived in the Black Forest), collect the fir branches and then make our own Advent wreath. This was quite a lot work, but we children always enjoyed it. You can find instructions on how to make your own (albeit artificial)

Advent wreath at www.inside-munich.com/crafts.

Each Sunday, one of the candles is lit. One candle on the first Sunday of Advent, two candles on the second, three candles on the third, until the Sunday before Christmas Eve when you light all four candles. This is a nice way to see how Christmas is approaching, especially for kids who don't have a feeling for time yet.

There's even a German poem to describe the burning of the four candles and the arrival of the baby Jesus Christ:

Advent, Advent, ein Lichtlein brennt.
Erst eins, dann zwei, dann drei, dann vier,
dann steht das Christkind vor der Tür.

By the way, you should always light the same candles because you're not supposed to use the last one before the fourth Sunday of Advent. I know, this leaves the candles in different lengths, almost burning down the first candle while the last one is still untouched. This made me really anxious as a kid, because I always wanted all of the candles to have the same lengths.

2.2 Advent Calendar - *Adventskalender*

Another very nice custom is the *Adventskalender*, the Advent calendar. It's mostly for kids, but many adults, including me, want one too.

The simplest form is an A3 format box (similar size to tabloid) with 24 little doors and a Christmas scene printed on it. Behind each of the 23 small and 1 bigger door a little chocolate is hidden. Every day, the children are allowed to open one of the doors and eat the chocolate. This keeps them in sweet anticipation for Christmas Eve and also helps them to realize how long they still have to wait.

As for me I became a master in opening the doors, eating the chocolates and artfully closing the doors again, so you almost couldn't tell the difference. But what a disappointment, when the doors I was allowed to open days later were already empty!

While the store-bought Adventskalender are nice, it's even nicer to make your own one. It's actually very easy to do, the hardest part is to come up with 24 ideas for little gifts.

You can use 24 small cloth pouches, write the number on it, and put little gifts inside. If you want to invest more time and are good at crafting, you can use toilet paper rolls to make 24 cute little Santas and hide the presents inside.

Here's an example of how these hand-crafted Advent calenders look like (the text is in German, but you'll get the idea by looking at the pictures): http://www.kindergeschenk-idee.com/adventskalender-basteln.html

3   St. Nicholas Day - Nikolaustag

Another kid's favorite is St. Nicholas Day on December 6. Saint Nicholas is a figure similar to Santa Claus, and now the two are intermingled.

Saint Nicholas was the Bishop of Myra in the 4th century, who later became a Catholic saint because of the many miracles attributed to him. Throughout his lifetime, he had the habit of secret gift-giving, such as putting coins in the shoes of those who left them out for him, a practice celebrated on December 6.

This practice would become the model for the modern Nikolaus or Santa Claus. In Germany, Nikolaus does both, secret and overt gift-giving. Children place their boots beside the door on the evening before St. Nicholas Day, hoping to find them filled with Mandarin oranges, nuts, chocolates or little toys in the morning.

But there's another, even more thrilling Nikolaus tradition, and this is when St. Nicholas and his dark companion Knecht Ruprecht (or also called Krampus) personally come to visit the homes of the families. This visit is one of the highlights for little kids who still believe in Nikolaus, but it's also a quite frightening experience since he carries a golden book with all the bad things you did during the past year.

The door rings, kids are asked to open it, and there he is: the friendly Nikolaus with his golden book and a bag full of gifts, and the not-so-friendly Knecht Ruprecht with a stone and a stick. Children will be asked whether they've been good throughout the year, and after they promise to behave well in the next year and possibly recite a Christmas poem or sing a Christmas carol, they're rewarded with gifts from Nikolaus's big bag. Knecht Ruprecht usually never has to jump in since all kids promise to behave in order to get their gifts!

One of the most famous stories about the historic character Bishop Nicholas is this one:

A poor man had three daughters, but could not afford a proper dowry for them. Back then the future for an unmarried woman was bleak to say the least and the three girls were desperate. Nicholas decided to help them with a secret gift and visited their house under the cover of night and threw three purses (one for each daughter) filled with gold coins through the window opening into the house.

4   German Christmas Markets

Christmas markets, also called Weihnachtsmarkt, Christkindlmarkt or Adventsmarkt, are one of my favorite German Christmas traditions. They bring that special magic to the holiday season and even though they've often been imitated, nothing gets close to an authentic German Christmas market.

They usually open on the Friday before the first Sunday in Advent and close one or two days before Christmas Eve. Even the smallest town has its own fair, maybe not for the whole Advent time, but at least for one weekend or two.

The oldest markets date back to the 14th century. Originally, they were real markets where you could stock up on produce for the long winter. In most parts of Germany it was the last regular market for a few months (until the farmers had new produce in the spring), thus these last markets of the season became more and more a special event.

Nowadays, they're a place to gather with friends and family to eat and drink and to buy gifts with little remembrances of the markets of the past.

Our main reasons to go to the Christmas marts is to meet friends and enjoy the festive mood. We usually meet and just stand around chatting and having a good time. This might seem rather strange to you because the weather during December can be very cold in Germany. So why on earth would we like to stand around outside freezing like crazy?

Well, this question cannot be answered easily, but there are several strategies to avoid getting too cold. Apart from wearing warm clothes, of course. One of them is to drink Glühwein (mulled wine).

Once you're at the Christmas market and have walked around to see all the stands, you surely will get hungry very soon and therefore half of the booths sell food (or drinks). The typical offerings are traditional things like bratwurst (sausage), but also German Christmas foods like the famous Lebkuchen (gingerbread), fruitcake, Stollen (bread with fruit in it), pancakes with chocolate, chocolate-dipped fruits, sugar-roasted almonds, sweet chestnuts and many more goodies.

4.1 Famous German Christmas Markets

There are thousands of Christmas markets in Germany, probably most of them are worth visiting. Below you can find my compilation of the most famous ones. If you ever visit Germany in December, make sure to visit at least one of them.

Rothenburg ob der Tauber

This town is the epitome of the Christmas spirit. In the medieval city center you find a comparatively small market called *Reiterlesmarkt* as well as the famous year-round Christmas village by Käthe Wohlfahrt. You can read all about Käthe Wohlfahrt Christmas company in a separate chapter.

Cologne – Köln

Who hasn't heard of Cologne? This ancient city is located on the banks of the Rhine river and attracts millions of visitors every year – not only for Christmas. As with every big city in Germany, Cologne has more than one Weihnachtsmarkt. The biggest one is right in front of the majestic Cologne Cathedral (Kölner Dom). Talk about a breathtaking scenery for your Christmas shopping.

Dresden

The market in Dresden is called *Strietzelmarkt*, which refers to the world-famous Dresdner Christstollen, a Christmas bread specific to Dresden. The market dates back to 1434, making it one of the oldest ones in Germany.

It has splendidly retained its traditional, old-fashioned charm in spite of the many visitors who come here every year. The main things to buy are the wood carvings from the nearby Erzgebirge region.

Extra Tip: When you visit Dresden, don't miss the breathtaking Grünes Gewölbe (green vault), one of the most impressive treasure chambers in Europe. Tickets have to be booked well in advance because only a certain number of visitors are allowed in.

Munich

I might be biased because I live here, but we do have astounding Christmas markets.

The biggest and most famous one is at Marienplatz. It's big, beautiful and crowded. But if you want something unique, a Weihnachtsmarkt you won't find anywhere else, then the **Kripperlmarkt** (manger market) just a few minutes from Marienplatz, is where you should head.

Here, you can buy anything and everything you might need for an authentic wooden crib for your home. Most wood carvings come from the small Bavarian town of Oberammergau and the Erzgebirge region. Come here and marvel!

Frankfurt

The main Weihnachtsmarkt at Römerberg is also among the oldest ones in Germany dating back as far as 1393. With more than 200 stalls it's also a really big one. Even if you're not planning to stay in Frankfurt, you might be able to arrange a short visit to the Christmas market when changing flights at the airport.

Nuremberg – Nürnberg

For me this is the definitely the best one. First, it's huge: officially it's held at the Hauptmarkt, but actually it stretches far beyond that area and almost across the whole city center. Second, you can buy the world-famous Nürnberger Lebkuchen (gingerbread) directly from the source. And I can tell you they taste yummy! Third, if you like mulled wine, try *Heidelbeerwein* (blueberry wine); this has been the first place I tried it. What a difference! No way to return to ordinary Glühwein.

5   Christmas Eve

In contrast to other countries like the U.S., we exchange gifts on Christmas Eve or Holy Night and not on Christmas Day. But even though we celebrate the Holy Night, we still want to have lots of time to play with our new toys, and therefore the 25th (Christmas Day) and 26th (Boxing Day) are public holidays.

Traditionally, Christmas is a family event. You will hear many German families complain about the travel stress they're having as many cross the country to first visit one side of the family and on the next day the other side.

On December 24 most shops and companies close around noon, so basically everyone has half a day off. Even though celebrations differ because each family has its own unique traditions, let me tell you how a typical Christmas Eve could look like.

Many families start to decorate the Christmas tree on that day. Everyone gathers around the tree, and while one or two dedicated persons decorate it, the others probably do some last-minute gift wrapping, bake cookies or prepare dinner, all of this accompanied by Christmas carols (usually from the radio or DVD). Sometimes, the children are allowed to participate, sometimes they have to wait outside (because they believe in the Christ child who delivers gifts).

When darkness sets in, the living room with the Christmas tree is closed, and everyone has to wait outside while the head of the family makes last minute arrangements.

I remember anxiously waiting for the ringing of the little bell, which was the sign for us children to be allowed back into the living room to finally get our presents. When the door opened, we would stand there in awe and stare at the festively decorated and lit-up tree. (Many families still use real candles).

After the *Bescherung* (gift giving) the family sits down to have a light dinner. In my family this used to be canapés or trout. The real holiday feast is eaten on Christmas Day and again on Boxing Day. After dinner we like to sit down together to talk, sing Christmas carols and play with our presents.

It's a custom to attend the midnight service at church, but nowadays, teenagers and twenty-somethings also go to the movies or a night club after the *Bescherung*.

6   Christ Child – Christkind

What would Christmas be without the presents? And who delivers them? Well, here in Germany traditionally it's not the *Weihnachtsmann* (Santa Claus) who comes through the chimney and brings presents to the kids. It's the *Christkind*. The Christkind is not actually Baby Jesus, but a child version of the spirit of Christmas, much like Father Christmas is the adult version.

As I've never seen him, I can only tell you what my grandmother said about the Christ child: He looks like an angel with blond hair and huge white wings and flies through the skies.

Whenever he spots a well-behaved child, he quickly enters the living room of that family through the window (therefore it's good to leave the window open a little bit) to deliver the presents.

My grandma told me every year that she had seen the Christ child flying nearby our house, and I remember how I stared outside to catch a glimpse. But unfortunately, I never managed to see him myself.

Mysteriously enough, though, a short time later I heard a little bell ringing inside our living room and knew that once again, I was too late, and the Christ child had already delivered my presents without my being able to see him.

The presents were laid down under the tree, and the bell ringing gave the signal to us kids to storm the living room.

There was the tree, beautifully decorated and lit up with candles (real ones) and *Wunderkerzen* (sparklers). Now, the painful waiting would begin. For some reason my parents wouldn't allow us to run straight for the presents and rip them open all at once, but they gave each of us two Wunderkerzen to hold. The light was shut off, and we stood there singing a Christmas carol and holding the burning sparklers in our hands.

As soon as they had burned down, my sister and I would jump forward to switch on the lights again and then go for the presents. In my family, though, it was customary that one person would sit near the tree and pick up the presents, read the name on it, give it to that person, and everyone would watch as it was opened. Talk about waiting.

But there are other customs as well: Some families first distribute all the presents and then each person starts ripping them open, which takes the joy out of looking at the faces of everyone when opening their presents. But I guess it's how you're used to doing is what you like best.

7   Christmas Tree – Weihnachtsbaum

The Christmas tree is a true German tradition. It was used here for the first time in the 15th century, and since then this wonderful custom has spread over the world. Here, we are very attached to our Christmas tree customs, and a German Christmas without a fir (or spruce or pine) tree is simply unthinkable.

Traditionally, the Christmas tree is decorated on Christmas Eve, prior to the evening feast and stays up until January 6, the day of Epiphany (the last day of Christmas when the Magi arrived at the manger). In contrast to this all the public Christmas trees are decorated long before, usually on the 1st day of Advent. Many of them are outdoors in public squares, but also every major shop, company, church, etc. has its own Christmas tree.

The german word Weihnachtsbaum consists of three words: Weih – Nacht – Baum.

Baum means tree, *Nacht* is night and *Weih* means holy. Tree of the Holy Night.

7.1   *Cutting the tree – Weihnachtsbaum schlagen*

Nowadays, there's a whole industry that caters to the need for fir and pine trees. Millions of trees are grown on farms for the sole purpose of being used as Christmas trees.

During Advent there are tree stands at basically every corner. But if you don't want just any Christmas tree, but your special tree, then you can make buying your tree a special event. Families, especially with children, spend an entire day visiting a pick-your-own farm.

The farm provides saws to cut the tree, and usually the children are allowed to choose, but the father cuts the tree and brings it to the car. Many pick-your-own farms make a special occasion out of getting a Christmas tree and provide food and drink as well as performances and educational exhibitions about the tree-farming industry.

If you ever have the chance to visit Germany during Advent, you definitely should visit one of the Christmas tree farms (even if you don't want to buy a tree) with your children.

8   Christmas Ornaments and Decorations

In Germany we like to decorate our homes for Christmas. Some ornaments have been handed down for generations and are the pride of each family. Still, we love to buy at least one more Christmas decoration every year.

Here are the most commonly used ones:

Glass balls

Glass balls (*Glaskugeln*) are some of the most dazzling ornaments around. They're typically hand-painted with various designs and often feature traditional German Christmas sayings, highlight a Bible scene or some winter landscape like in the picture above.

While many of the ornaments are locally made, there are prominent designers like Käthe Wohlfahrt. Mostly, we don't hang those big glass balls on our trees, but in the windows, and it really is a nice sight to look at those glass ornaments when they shine in the light.

Straw star – Strohsterne

We just love straw stars. You'll see them on almost every Christmas tree. In the photo below you can see a stall at the Christmas market selling nothing but straw stars.

Of course, you can also make your own. When I was a kid, we made *Strohsterne* every year for Christmas. It's a lot of fun, and though they never look as perfect as the bought ones, they're even more special.

The tradition says that straw represents the manger of Jesus, but the more plausible explanation might be that straw was a very common material centuries ago. Even the poorest families could get their hands on straw to make their own Christmas decorations. By the way, don't take the word "star" literally, a straw star can also be an angel, reindeer, heart, snowflake or any other shape.

Here's a very simple instruction to make your own straw stars:

You need 4 straws and white twine.

- Cut straws into halves
- put 2 of them in form of a cross over each other. Press tightly in the middle
- make another cross and put over the first (slightly shifted)
- use the twine to stabilize them by winding it around the crossing of the straws above, below, above, below ....
- make a nod and cut the twine
- cut the ends of the straws to form little tops

Now you have a simple star with 8 ends. To make a double straw with 16 ends, repeat the steps above and then place the second star slightly shifted above the first one.

If you feel creative, use different colored straws.

Wood Carvings

Wood carvings are another favorite for our Christmas tree decorations. Traditionally, religious figures like angels, Joseph and Mary or even a little crib are hung upon the tree.

Another traditional wood carving, although not used as a tree ornament but for the table, are wooden pyramids with candles that turn the sails on the pyramid when the candles are lit. As a kid I loved to sit in front of the pyramid and watch the sails turn, and I always asked myself, why they didn't burn. The moving propellers make wonderful shadows on the walls and ceiling, adding even more to the cozy Christmas spirit.

Candles and Lights

Many families including mine still use real candles to put on the Christmas tree; it gives a totally different atmosphere. Yes, many families have changed to electric lights for convenience and security reasons, but I think the candles are much more like Christmas.

Of course, there are a few things to keep in mind when using candles.

You have to choose where to carefully place them (not near the straw stars), and you need to keep a fire extinguisher or bucket of water close to the tree. Also, you should only use real candles with a fresh tree that's still wet and juicy.

Apart from the candles for the tree, we love to decorate our house with candles in all shapes, sizes and colors. Candles and Christmas just belong together.

Christmas Mugs

Get an authentic Christmas mug from one of the German Christmas markets to keep the Christmas spirit alive for years to come.

The stands that sell hot drinks usually serve the drink in a commemorative mug. The cups are specifically designed for the Christmas market. They feature a unique logo or emblem, the year and something along the lines of "*xxx Weihnachtsmarkt*". The mugs are given out, with a 2 Euro deposit, so that customers will return the cup at the end of their drink. But you can also choose to keep your mug as a German Christmas gift and have a unique and practical souvenir. Of course, you can also buy new and clean ones, so you don't have to carry the sticky Glühwein mug with you. This is a nice German Christmas souvenir for your friends at home.

Music box – Spieldose

Many booths in the Christmas markets sell unique, handmade music boxes featuring every winter theme and design. Spieldosen are one of the most iconic items from Germany and are sure to be a keepsake in your family's Christmas collection. Käthe Wohlfahrt's world-famous company even started with a simple music box. Now you see, how well-liked those *Spieldose* are.

Nutcracker – Nussknacker

Nuts are, traditionally, important winter food with a long shelf-life. They provided important nutrients at a time of the year when fresh produce wasn't available. This is how the nutcrackers became synonym with Christmas season.

Nutcrackers are maybe the most typical German Christmas ornament. They are made of wood and carefully painted. The most usual type is a king or soldier, but you can get them in all professions now. Bakers, hunters, doctors and even golfers are available.

They come in all sizes as well, the most common are the small ones about 25cm (10 inches) to put on the table or the windowsill. But you can also get them in human size.

Even though they still can crack nuts, these sometimes very expensive pieces serve merely decorative purposes.

One heroic nutcracker soldier even made it into Tchaikovsky's ballet, The Nutcracker, based on a German Christmas fairy tale written by E.T.A. Hoffmann.

What we don't use

Some things that are very popular in other countries but you rarely see in Germany, are bows and ties. Lametta (tinsel) used to be very popular in the '70s and '80s but is rarely used nowadays. Artificial snow to top the trees is also an exception.

One more thing we generally don't use are plastic trees: a German Christmas tree has to be a real fir or pine.

9   Christmas Dishes

The holiday season is the time for indulging, and it starts early in December with all kinds of cookies. Three of my favorite cookie recipes and one special recipe from my friend Rita are in the next chapter, but first lets discuss the "typical" Christmas food and drinks.

9.1   *Food*

On Holy Night we don't eat that much; the real feast together with relatives is eaten on Christmas Day (December 25).

The traditional food is Christmas goose with dumplings and red cabbage. Usually, this is prepared for the whole family. A goose takes many hours in the oven until it's ready. Many families also opt for a smaller duck instead of the goose.

9.2   *Spices*

The typical Christmas spices that everyone attributes to Christmas are clove and cinnamon. There's also plenty of sugar. You can smell the spices almost everywhere. They can be used in cookies, other sweets but also in drinks like Glüehwein.

9.3   *Drinks*

Glühwein (mulled wine)

The ubiquitous drink, of course, is Glühwein (mulled wine). It's hardly possible to get through December without drinking at least one mug. This is a German Christmas tradition and only available in winter: It's sweet red or white wine that's sweetened even more with sugar, cloves and cinnamon.

You can drink it "with Schuss" or "without Schuss," which means with a shot of schnapps or without. For beginners I strongly recommend the version without the liqueur!

Usually, you don't stop with only one, so it's a good idea, to eat some food before indulging in too much of our delicious Glühwein. Of course, you can also drink the kid-friendly version without alcohol called Kinderpunsch.

Super-Simple Glühwein Recipe:

Use sweet red wine (if it isn't sweet enough, you have to add sugar). Put into a pot and heat over low heat on the stove. Add cloves, cinnamon and ginger. Keep on low heat for 3-5 minutes while constantly stirring. If the liquid starts boiling, the alcohol will evaporate.

Bowle (Rumtopf)

Bowle is a rum-based drink that contains sparkling wine and fruit. Popular fruits to use are strawberries and mandarin oranges. I remember my grandmother would make bowle every year for Christmas, but we children were only allowed to take one sip and then had to drink our own bowle made of sparkling water.

Feuerzangenbowle

Another typical drink for Christmas and New Year's is *Feuerzangenbowle* (brandy punch or burnt punch). Even though the recipe has been known for at least 200 years, it only became popular when a movie of the same name came out in the 1940s starring the famous German actor Heinz Rühmann.

Since then, the Feuerzangenbowle has found its place in many German households during Christmas time.

Of course, you can buy Feuerzangenbowle in the Christmas markets, but the true fun lies in making it yourself, which is not as complicated as it seems and is always a lot of fun. We even managed to make one in China, where it was difficult enough to hunt down the ingredients, and we even had to create our own sugar loaf (Zuckerhut).

Not-so-simple Feuerzangenbowle Recipe

Ingredients:

- 2 liter (1/2 gallon) red wine
- ½ liter (2 quarts) orange juice
- 1 organic orange
- 1 organic lemon
- 1 cinnamon stick
- 6 cloves
- 1 sugar loaf
- 350 ml (1 ½ cups) rum, at least 50% alcohol

Cut the orange and lemon in pieces (including the peel).

Heat red wine in a pot and add cinnamon and cloves. Keep the mixture just below simmering for a few minutes. Then put the pot onto a teapot warmer. Add oranges and lemons.

Now you will need some kind of metallic (non burnable) holder that is put on top of the pot with your wine mixture. Put the sugar loaf into the holder and soak with rum. Now light the sugar loaf with matches and the rum starts burning (this is why you need at least 50% alcohol, otherwise it won't burn).

The burning sugar starts dripping into the bowle pot below. Keep adding rum until all of the sugar loaf has dissolved.

Stir and serve in glasses!

One word of warning: Never, ever hold the rum bottle into the flame.

10   German Christmas Cookies

The holiday season without cookies just wouldn't be the same.

You can buy them everywhere, industrially manufactured and packaged Christmas cookies in the supermarkets, hand-made exclusive ones from bakeries, but the most fun, of course, is to bake them yourself.

Baking *Weihnachtsplätzchen* is the German Christmas tradition nobody wants to miss. In fact, even though most people complain about the fattening holiday season, almost everyone bakes their own cookies. And you rarely ever see a person refusing to eat an offered cookie.

Starting from December 1, your neighbors and colleagues offer you their newest cookie creations and offices smell of freshly baked Lebkuchen, cinnamon stars and other German Christmas cookies.

When I was a kid, we used to bake *Vanillekipferl* (almond-vanilla crescents) and *Ausstecherle* (done with cookie cutters), which always drove my mother crazy because my sister and I would eat the dough instead of forming the cookies. Afterwards, we were usually sick from eating too much dough and didn't want to eat the baked cookies anymore.

My husband and I started a few years ago with our own "Cookie Production". Every year we bake one or two evergreens and try at least one new and exotic recipe.

I have tried to convert the measures to the U.S. system, but you might want to use the metric measures if possible, just to be on the safe side.

10.1 Cinammon Stars - Zimtsterne

My all-time favorites, though, are cinnamon stars (*Zimtsterne*). I'm really reluctant to share them and don't want to give any of those delicious little sweet treats away. Below is my favorite cinnamon star recipe.

I used to think they must be very complicated to bake because they taste so heavenly. But in fact, they're quite easy and straightforward to prepare.

Cinnamon and cloves are the typical flavors associated with Christmas in Germany; therefore, Zimtsterne are not only my favorite Christmas cookies but for many others as well.

The only thing you need before starting, is a star-shaped cookie cutter. If you don't have one (or more), you can usually buy it at any supermarket nearby. Just not shortly before the holidays. Last year, we needed some last-minute cookie cutters and learned they were sold out in at least three shops!

Ingredients

- 250g (a little more than 1 cup) ground almonds
- 3 egg whites
- 250g (a little more than 1 cup) powdered sugar
- 2 teaspoons ground cinnamon
- 100g (little less than ½ cup) sugar

Directions

Beat the egg whites until stiff. Fold in powdered sugar until thoroughly mixed.

Set 4 tablespoons of egg white mixture apart for topping.

Mix ground almonds and cinnamon. Add the rest of the egg white mixture to ground almonds and knead until dough isn't liquid anymore.

Sprinkle your work surface with sugar and roll out the dough to about 0,5 cm (less than 1/4 inch) thick.

Important: Don't use flour for sprinkling because this will change the consistency of your dough and make the cinnamon stars taste "floury."

Cover your baking tray with baking (parchment) paper.

Cut out cinnamon stars with cookie cutter and carefully place onto baking tray.

Brush the cookies with the reserved egg white mixture to make the topping.

Bake at 150°C/300°F until slightly golden. Be careful not to burn your cinnamon stars; the topping should remain white.

Makes two batches.

10.2   Almond crescents - Vanillekipferl

Who doesn't like those yummy almond crescents? I always wondered why they're called "vanilla" if they taste like almonds? In German the name is derived from the vanilla sugar you use to powder them. Anyhow, they're super-easy to make, and even small kids can roll the crescents or at least something similar. The shapes might differ, the taste's the same!

Ingredients

- 210g (slightly less than 1 cup) butter
- 100g (little less than ½ cup) sugar
- 100g (little less than ½ cup) almonds, unpeeled and ground
- 250g (2 cups) flour
- salt
- 1 tablespoon vanilla extract
- 50g (1.5 oz) powdered sugar
- 2 tablespoons vanilla sugar

Directions

Stir butter and sugar until frothy. Slowly add almonds, flour, vanilla flavor and a dash of salt to make dough.

Put dough 30 minutes into fridge to cool.

Cut dough into quarters and form rolls. Cut down 1cm (a little more than 1/3 inch) slices from the rolls and form little crescents.

Grease baking sheet or use parchment paper and put the crescents onto the baking sheet.

Important: Don't place them too near together, because the dough will expand while baking.

Preheat oven to 180°C/360°F and bake for approximately 12-15 minutes, until golden.

Mix powdered sugar with vanilla sugar in a bowl.

Carefully remove the crescents from the baking sheet and roll them in the sugar.

Let cool down on a cooling rack and eat!

10.3 Ausstecherle – Butter Cookies

Butter cookies is a basic cookie recipe you can use to let your creativity go wild. Depending on the topping, they taste different every time. They can differ in shape (use whatever cookie cutters you feel like or even make your own) and in taste. You can really splash on decorations: chocolate, sugar sprinkles, food coloring, jam, crushed nuts.... there's nothing you can't use.

Ingredients

- 250g (2 cups) flour
- 70g (2 oz.) butter
- 125g (½ cup) sugar
- 1 egg
- 1/3 package baking powder or baking soda
- 1/3 package vanilla sugar (vanilla bean mixed into the sugar)
- egg yolk
- milk
- Decorations: Colored sugar sprinkles, chocolate sprinkles, jam, edible pearls, whatever you like

Directions

Stir butter, sugar, vanilla sugar and egg until frothy.

Slowly pour the flour while constantly kneading to make dough.

Put dough into fridge for 30 minutes to cool. Dust the working area and a rolling pin with flour and roll out the dough 3-4 mm (1/8-inch) thin.

Now the fun part begins: Use cutters with Christmas motifs to cut out the cookies and place them onto a greased baking tray.

Brush the butter cookies with egg yolk (or egg yolk mixed with milk) and decorate them with whatever decorations you have. You can be as creative as you like making faces, different colors, etc. This is a wonderful task, especially for kids.

Preheat oven to 180°C/360°F and bake for approximately 10 minutes or until golden.

10.4   Coconut Macaroons

This recipe was provided by my friend Rita, the owner of www.germany-insider-facts-com. If you want to know more about Germany, her website is a great source of information.

Ingredients for approximately 35 to 40 macaroons

150g (3/4 cup) sugar

150g desiccated coconut

1 pinch salt

2 egg whites

If you like you can season with 1 pinch cinnamon and/or 1 drop almond essence.

Preparation

Preheat the oven to 140°C (275°F), if you have a fan oven 120°C (250°F)

Carefully separate yolks from egg whites.

Whisk the egg whites with an electric mixer at the highest speed until it gets stiff, add the sugar and spices step by step.

Fold in the coconut.

Use 2 teaspoons to form small piles, put them either on round baking wafers, or on a baking sheet lined with parchment.

Bake for about 25 minutes. Remove the sheet from the oven when the macaroons start getting golden, they should be soft inside.

Let the coconut macaroons cool down on a rack. Guten Appetit!

10.5 More German Christmas Cookies

Marzipan

Marzipan or almond paste can be eaten alone but most often is part of some cookie or bread.

Christmas Stollen, Weihnachtsstollen or Christstollen

There are many kinds of Christmas Stollen in Germany, but the most famous is definitely the *Dresdner Stollen*. The first reference to the Dresdner Stollen dates back to the 15th century, when it still was a hard and dry cake made with oil instead of butter.

Over the centuries the Stollen changed from that dry and tasteless bread to a sweet fruitcake containing dried fruit, candied fruit, marzipan and/or nuts and covered with powdered sugar.

The tradition of Christmas Stollen reputedly started in Dresden (that's why the residents claim the Dresdner Stollen is the only true Stollen in the world, and all others are simply copies) with the legendary celebration of King Friedrich August I, better known as August the Strong of Saxony and his 24,000 guests in 1730.

Apparently, he ordered a huge Stollen, and every one of his guests had at least one piece of cake. In remembrance of this occasion the city of Dresden celebrates the Stollen Festival every year on the Saturday before the second Sunday of Advent, and the cakes made there weigh between three and four tonne (3000 kg or 6000 pounds).

It's a real show: The Giant Dresdner Stollen is put in a carriage and taken through the streets of the city to the Christmas market, cut in front of hundreds of spectators and directly sold from the Stollen cart.

The legend has it that the Stollen in its typical shape and with its white layer of icing sugar is the symbol of the Christ Child wrapped in diapers.

Gingerbread -Lebkuchen

What would Christmas be without Lebkuchen, especially Nürnberger Lebkuchen?

Lebkuchen (similar to gingerbread cookies) apparently were invented by medieval monks in Franconia, Germany, in the 13th century. They're also known to have a variety of different ingredients and therefore tastes.

Lebkuchen range in taste from spicy to sweet and come in a variety of shapes with round the most common. The sweet ones are also known as honey cake (*Honigkuchen*), the spicy ones as pepper cake (*Pfefferkuchen*).

The ingredients may include honey, aniseed, coriander, cloves, ginger, cardamom, allspice, nuts including almonds, hazelnuts and walnuts, or candied fruit.

11   Christmas Carols

Christmas carols are an important part of the holiday season. There are thousands of them, and each year new ones are composed. I could give you the names and lyrics of at least a dozen traditional songs, but I believe the three below are the most well-known carols. If you learn only these three, you're prepared for any Germany Christmas celebration. The notes can be found on YouTube or Amazon without difficulty.

11.1   *Stille Nacht, Heilige Nacht*

Silent Night is probably the most famous Christmas carol all over the world. It's not really German, but Austrian. It was created in 1818 in Oberndorf a small town near Salzburg by Franz Xaver Gruber and Joseph Mohr.

By the way, until 1816, Oberndorf belonged to Bavaria (Germany) and then was given to Salzburg (Austria), so the song missed being German for two years.

From then on, this carol took its course all over Europe and the world. Nowadays the lyrics have been translated into more than 100 languages. It truly is the epitome of Christmas.

Here are the German lyrics to it:

Stille Nacht! Heilige Nacht!

Alles schläft, Einsam wacht

Nur das traute hochheilige Paar.

Holder Knab' im lockigen Haar.

Schlaf in himmlischer Ruh!

Schlaf in himmlischer Ruh!

Stille Nacht! Heilige Nacht!

Gottes Sohn, O! wie lacht

Lieb aus Deinem göttlichen Mund,
Da schlägt uns die rettende Stund.
Jesus! in deiner Geburt!
Jesus! in deiner Geburt!

Stille Nacht! Heilige Nacht!
Die der Welt Heil gebracht,
Aus des Himmels goldenen Höh'n
Uns der Gnaden Fülle läßt seh'n:
Jesu in Menschengestalt!
Jesu in Menschengestalt!

Stille Nacht! Heilige Nacht!
Wo sich heut alle Macht
Väterlicher Liebe ergoß
Und als Bruder Huldvoll umschloß
Jesus die Völker der Welt!
Jesus die Völker der Welt!

11.2　*Ihr Kinderlein Kommet*

A very easy song that calls all children to come and visit Jesus' crib. I remember I had to sing this song in the third grade during music class in front of the whole classroom. I'm a really bad singer, but with a little help from the teacher, even I managed to sing it correctly.

The text was written by the catholic priest Christoph von Schmid 1811 and the music by Franz Xaver Luft in 1837.

Ihr Kinderlein kommet o kommet doch all

zur Krippe her kommet in Bethlehems Stall

und seht was in dieser hochheiligen Nacht

der Vater im Himmel für Freude uns macht

O seht in der Krippe im nächtlichen Stall

seht hier bei des Lichtleins hellglänzendem Strahl

in reinlichen Windeln das himmlische Kind

viel schöner und holder als Engel es sind

Da liegt es das Kindlein auf Heu und auf Stroh

Maria und Joseph betrachten es froh

die redlichen Hirten knien betend davor

hoch oben schwebt jubelnd der Engelein Chor

O beugt wie die Hirten anbetend die Knie

erhebet die Hände und danket wie sie

stimmt freudig ihr Kinder wer sollt sich nicht freun

stimmt freudig zum Jubel der Engel mit ein

11.3   O Tannenbaum

This is my favorite Christmas carol, it talks about the Christmas tree that never loses its leaves but stays green in summer as well as in winter.

It is one of the oldest Christmas songs, and dates back to the 16th century. It's not exactly clear when and where the first version of this song was created. Some sources name Melchior Frank and his volks song "Ach Tannenbaum". It became a Christmas carol in 1824, when Ernst Anschütz added two more verses.

O Tannenbaum, O Tannenbaum
Wie treu sind deine Blätter
Du grünst nicht nur zur Sommerzeit
Nein auch im Winter wenn es schneit
O Tannenbaum, o Tannenbaum
Wie treu sind deine Blätter

O Tannenbaum, O Tannenbaum
Du kannst mir sehr gefallen
Wie oft hat nicht zur Weihnachtszeit
Ein Baum von dir mich hoch erfreut
O Tannenbaum, o Tannenbaum
Du kannst mir sehr gefallen

O Tannenbaum, O Tannenbaum
Dein Kleid will mich was lehren
Die Hoffnung und Beständigkeit
Gibt Mut und Kraft zu jeder Zeit
O Tannenbaum, o Tannenbaum
Dein Kleid will mich was lehren

12   Nativity Scene/Manger

According to the history, Saint Francis of Assisi was the first one to use a manger in 1223, and from there this tradition started to spread through Italy, Spain and Germany. Today, nativity scenes decorate all Roman Catholic and many Protestant churches in Germany during Advent. Also many families started to have their own mangers at home.

A Nativity scene usually consists of the stable and several figurines. The stable may range in size from 10 inches (15 cm) to life-size and usually has three closed walls, with only the front side open.

The minimum number of figurines you need are the Holy Family, Mary, Joseph and the infant Jesus in his crib. Of course, you can add as many other characters as you want: ox and donkey, cherubs, angels, the Three Wise Men, shepherds, shepherd dog, sheep and camels.

As tradition has it, you're not supposed to put little Jesus into his crib before Christmas Eve, and the Three Wise Men have to wait for their appearance until Epiphany.

A crib or nativity scene is the ultimate German Christmas tradition, especially in Southern Germany where most people are still Roman Catholics.

Many young families start out with a small, basic manger, with just the stable and the Holy Family, and then year after year they buy one more character until they have a huge manger, that almost doesn't fit into their living rooms anymore.

Most of the figurines are intricate and unique woodcarvings from Oberammergau (near the Alps) or the Erzgebirge region. If you visit one of our Christmas markets, you can appreciate the sheer beauty of these woodcarvings and also buy yourself or someone special a wonderful gift.

13   Epiphany or Twelfth Night – Heilige Drei Könige

Epiphany is held on January 6 and celebrates the visit of the Three Wise Men (Magi) to the baby Jesus. It's a public holiday in some parts of Germany, but not everywhere.

A nice custom tied to Epiphany is the *Sternsinger* (carolers, literally star singers). Kids dress up as the Three Wise Men and their entourage and wander from house to house, singing Christmas carols. When they're finished, you give them a small donation for charity, and in turn the children in their role as Wise Men bless your home.

This is a Catholic tradition, celebrated only in the primarily catholic parts of Germany.

Then the Magi write the traditional letters **20*C+M+B+21** with chalk that has been consecrated by a priest above your door to ask for divine blessing.

The meaning of the inscription is said to be either:

- the names of the Three Kings: Caspar, Melchior and Balthazar or

- Christus mansionem benedicat (Latin for "Christ, bless this house")

- the * signifies the Star of Bethehem

- the three crosses +++ signify the Holy Trinity

- the numbers come from the new year that has just started, in my example 2021

Epiphany also indicates the end of the 12 days of Christmas, when traditionally, the Christmas tree gets "undecorated" and put away.

14 Other Traditions

There are many more Christmas traditions that are celebrated in certain parts of Germany and I'm certainly not able to list (or know) them all. Below are just some that I really like.

14.1 *Barbarazweig*

The Barbarazweig custom goes back to the legend about the merchant daughter Barbara in the 3rd century, who was baptized as a Christian against her father's wishes. He had her tortured and taken to the dungeon.

As the legend goes, a branch of cherry tree caught in her dress. During her time in the dungeon she desperately needed company and kept the branch as her only tie to the outside world. She diligently watered it with the water from her drinking cup. Miraculously, this same branch started to bloom on the day of her execution when she walked into the sunlight again.

Nowadays, people follow the custom of bringing branches of cherry, chestnut, apple or jasmine into the house on December 4 to bloom on Christmas Eve. With some precautions it always works, even though you can't predict how long it takes for the blossoms to appear. It may be a few days or three weeks.

If you want to follow the Barbarazweig tradition, cut stems with buds on a mild, non-freezing day. Put the branches for a few hours in cool water and then store them in a cool but not freezing room. When the buds start swelling, bring them into your living room and wait for the blossoms to appear.

14.2   Secret Santa - Wichteln

What would Christmas be without presents? Gift giving has become an important part of the holiday season, especially for kids.

One gift-giving custom that's very popular among bigger groups like school classes, clubs and other communities is the *Wichteln*.

First, all the names of the participants are written down and put into a bowl. Then, everyone takes one piece of paper (if you collect your own name you have to put it back). The name on the paper is the person you give a present to.

This way it's assured everyone gets a present and everyone has to buy only one gift, not many. Usually, a maximum price is set so everyone should have the same value of present when they're opened.

Usually, it's not revealed who the gift giver is, but of course, kids are clever and try to find out who the giver is by little signs like the wrapping paper, the handwriting on the box, etc.. It's almost more fun to run around and find out what the others got, try to find out who gave what to whom and finally even barter the gifts than the gift-giving itself.

15　Käthe Wohlfahrt Company

No book on German Christmas traditions would be complete without a reference to Käthe Wohlfahrt, the world-famous Christmas company in Rothenburg ob der Tauber.

Rothenburg is a charming little town with a medieval center and its Christmas market is one of the most romantic ones in Germany (see the chapter on Christmas markets). But what sets the town apart from every other one is the Käthe Wohlfahrt company, dedicated to making Christmas ornaments.

It all started in 1963 with a simple music box from the Erzgebirge. This music box with the Three Wise Men revolving around a manger scene on the turntable to the sounds of Stille Nacht (Silent Night) was the reason for founding a company that now exports the finest German Christmas ornaments to all the world.

Christmas Village and Workshop

Later on, the world-famous *Weihnachtsdorf* (Christmas Village) was opened in Rothenburg ob der Tauber. It's dedicated to selling nothing but Christmas items year-round. Even though it might seem strange for you to buy tree ornaments in July, you'll be caught up in the holiday spirit as soon as you enter the store and soon forget, that it's not yet December!

In the doorway "guarding" the Christmas Village stands a giant nutcracker in the likeness of　King Christian I. Posing for photographs with Christian is one of the the things you and your children shouldn't miss.

Most of the items are still made in the Christmas workshop (*Rothenburger Weihnachtswerkstatt*) in town, but there are also plenty of "made in China" items for sale. Make sure you check where your souvenirs really come from.

Christmas Museum

That little town with barely 10,000 inhabitants even has its own *Weihnachtsmuseum.* The Christmas museum is open year-round and invites you to embark on a journey to the past. Here, you will experience how Christmas was celebrated during past centuries. Learn the traditions and customs and be dazzled by the glittering glass balls, happy and grim Santas, uncountable nutcrackers and six-foot-tall pyramids.

16   New Years Eve - Silvester

The name Silvester comes from another saint: Pope Silvester I, who died December 31, 335.

While Christmas is the holiday to spend with your family, Silvester usually means celebrating with your friend. People go to big parties, either in their homes or a friend's home, but there are also many public events you can join. Some of the bigger parties slightly resemble the famous Fasching or carnival, with paper horns, party music, humorous speeches and performances, conga lines and lots and lots of food and drink.

When celebrating with friends, the most common food is **raclette.** A mini stove range is set on the table, surrounded by bowls of prepared, but uncooked ingredients like cheese, potatoes, meat, and vegetables. Each guest has his or her own little pan to cook a combination of the ingredients.

Another popular choice is **fondue**. Apart from the food being delicious and warming (remember you have to go out in the cold to watch the fireworks later on), these dishes are also very communicative and usually last for hours.

The black-and-white British comedy sketch *Dinner for One* is shown on German television, and at least half of the populations watches it every year with the same enthusiasm.

As for activities most people engage in things that are supposed to show the future, such as casting hot tin (Zinngießen) into cold water and guessing from the forms what the New Year will bring.

The main attraction though are fireworks at midnight. It's believed the fireworks are derived from the ancient year-end traditions, where people the bad spirits of the old year with a lot of noise, so they wouldn't cross over into the new year.

Unlike in the United States, fireworks are legal in Germany, and you can buy them starting a few days before Silvester in most shops and supermarkets. Basically every German male of age (and some females) buys his share of fireworks.

At midnight people flock to the streets and proudly detonate their ammunition until the air is full of smoke and the streets are awash with red paper detritus.

17   About the Author

Marion Kummerow was born and raised in the Black Forest, Germany, and has lived in many parts of Germany and the world until she settled down in Munich with her family.

Like many people she loves Christmas, and now she has put all of her knowledge about Christmas traditions and customs in Germany into this guidebook, including three of her favorite Christmas cookie recipes so her readers will know all about a real German Christmas.

I hope you enjoyed this book about German Christmas traditions. If you liked it, please recommend to a friend!

Also by Marion Kummerow

Munich's Ten Gorgeous Sights

Get the Most Out of Your Visit to Munich. This guide covers the 10 most spectacular places in Munich. Whether you're on a one-day, two-days or longer trip, the guidebook gives you the necessary information to make the most of your time. With this guide book you won't have to regret that you missed best spots, ran out of time or arrived at the museum just when it was about to close.

The Ultimate Guide to Oktoberfest

Everything you need to know about the Oktoberfest in Munich. Includes a detailed description of all beer tents, how to make a reservation and even secret tips on what to do if you don't have a reservation.

How to Rent an Apartment in Munich

The detailed step-by-step instructions in How to Rent an Apartment in Munich: Multiply Your Chances to Move into Your Dream Apartment map out your move to Germany for you. The glossary of German words helps you to communicate with lessors.

Made in the USA
Monee, IL
25 November 2024